INTERMEDIATE

Quiet Songs
of a
Holy Night

Beautiful Carols of the Nativity
for Organ and Piano

Lani Smith

Editor: Larry Shackley
Engraving: Linda Taylor
Cover Design: Katie Hufford

ISBN 978-0-7877-2509-9

Lorenz

A Lorenz Company • www.lorenz.com

From the Editor

For almost 50 years, the distinctive musical voice of Lani Smith (1934–2015) was a major part of our catalog. His vocal, keyboard, and instrumental arrangements numbered in the thousands, and are played in churches around the world every Sunday of the year.

The book you are about to play was Lani's final keyboard duet project for Lorenz. He passed away in June of 2015, just as we were about to work on the final engraving and proofreading of this collection. It's a beautiful addition to his legacy: eight elegant duets for the Christmas season, focusing on the quiet, meditative side of the story. We hope that these pieces will find a place in your worship services this year, and that you will join with us in remembering Lani Smith, an outstanding musician who has enriched the life of the church for decades.

Larry Shackley
Sacred Keyboard Editor

Contents

O Holy Night

Lani Smith
Tune: CANTIQUE DE NOËL
by **Adolphe Adam**

Ped. Light 16, 8, Sw. to Ped.

Duration: 2:30

70/1949L-3

The Holly and the Ivy

Lani Smith
Traditional English melody

Duration: 2:25

Sw. Flutes 8, 4, 2

Infant Holy, Infant Lowly

Lani Smith
Tune: **W ZLOBIE LEZY**
Traditional Polish Carol

Ped. Light 16, 8, Sw. to Ped.

Duration: 2:45

www.lorenz.com

O Jesu Sweet

Lani Smith
Tune: **O JESULEIN SÜSS**
Traditional German Melody

Ped. Light 16, 8

Duration: 3:25

Sw. Solo Flute 8

Sw. Solo Reed 8

What Child Is This?

Lani Smith
Tune: GREENSLEEVES
Traditional English Melody

Duration: 2:35

Ped. Light 8, 4, Sw. to Ped.

Joseph Dearest, Joseph Mine

Lani Smith
Tune: **RESONET IN LAUDIBUS**
Traditional German Melody

Duration: 1:55

36

70/1949L-36

Silent Night, Holy Night

Lani Smith
Tune: STILLE NACHT
by Franz Grüber

Peacefully ♩ = ca. 63

Piano — *p*

Organ — *p* { Sw. Light Strings 8, 4

Ped. Light 16, 8, Sw. to Ped.

Gt. Solo Prin. 8

Duration: 2:50

Peacefully ♩ = ca. 63

70/1949L-40

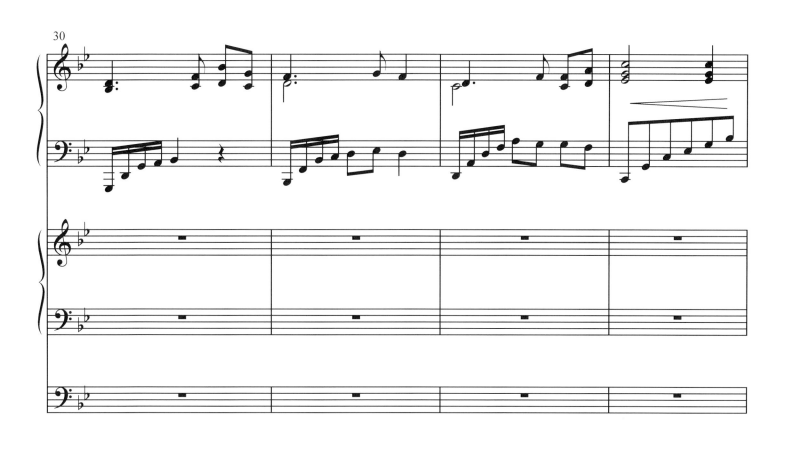

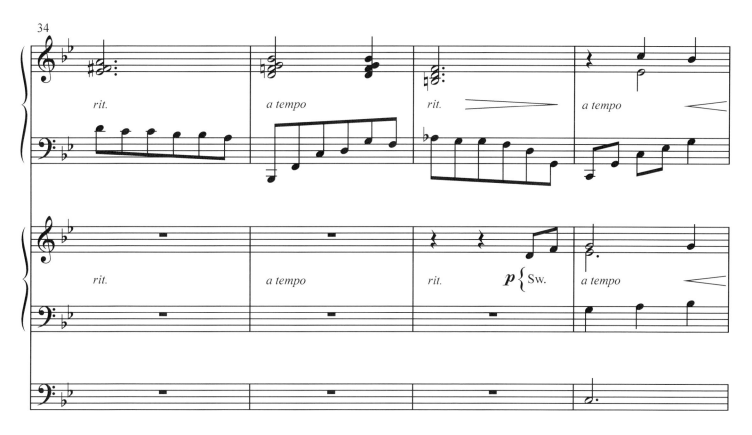

44

70/1949L-44

O Little Town of Bethlehem

Lani Smith
Tune: ST. LOUIS
by **Louis Redner**

Ped. Light 16, 8, Gt. to Ped.

Duration: 3:05

48

70/1949L-48

52